PRAISE FOR *CLYDE'S*

"*Clyde's* is *Sweat*'s foil. *Sweat* was long, grimly realistic, full of argument and instruction; *Clyde's* is short, buoyant, and atmospheric. *Sweat* asks a bleak question about whether work can sustain us; *Clyde's* offers a hopeful if fantastical answer . . . As the play lifts off into its final minutes, it enters a realm where conventional dramaturgy doesn't apply. These characters aren't heading for dramatic resolution. They're aiming for a place, reached via sensual delight, of reconnection and reawakening."

—HELEN SHAW, *VULTURE*

"*Clyde's* teases out its characters' backstories in a way that reflects on some of the grim systemic problems that *Sweat* also pondered: America's inadequate social safety net, a lack of second chances, capitalism's facility for exacerbating racial, ethnic, and class fault lines."

—CELIA WREN, *WASHINGTON POST*

"*Clyde's* is a down-at-heel diner kitchen, and also a bigger psychological space to ask questions about redemption, cruelty, control, love, and ambition . . . And it also asks whether liberation is possible via the art of making the perfect sandwich."

—TIM TEEMAN, *DAILY BEAST*

"Food for thought is on the menu, along with lots of laughs and a few tears in *Clyde's*, a richly entertaining and timely play . . . You can take the ending literally or poetically—chalk that up to Nottage's theatrical witchcraft."

—JOE DZIEMIANOWICZ, *NEW YORK THEATRE GUIDE*

"Despite the fact that this is a play about living with and through your mistakes, it's hysterical and real . . . In the end there is love and laughter, there is connection, there is possibility, and there is a sandwich."

—STEPHANIE MARCH, *MPLS.ST.PAUL MAGAZINE*

"Fast-paced and uproariously funny, *Clyde's* is a spicy feast for the senses . . . The characters that Nottage creates are vivid and just as enticing as the food, making you want to follow their stories when they leave the stage."

—SHERI FLANDERS, *CHICAGO SUN-TIMES*

"Clyde's sandwich shop is a kind of purgatory, the prison after they get out of prison. And yet within this hellscape, where nihilism or worse would be the obvious path, Montrellous still attracts disciples. For him, crafting the perfect sandwich is art, religion and, somehow, a way out. That others start dreaming of and demoing their perfect sandwiches is the play's great optimistic dare."

—LILY JANIAK, *SAN FRANCISCO CHRONICLE*

"Nationally renowned playwright Lynn Nottage has the gift of making us care deeply about her characters. Her empathy for the underclass is boundless, as we've seen in *Sweat*, in the memorably agonizing *Ruined*, and in the turn-of-the-century *Intimate Apparel*. The same is true in *Clyde's*, her latest play . . . This is a sweet, feel-good comedy with a fairytale ending; its characters are likely to linger in your mind, the way Nottage's characters do."

—JEAN SCHIFFMAN, *SFGATE*

"A fresh, compassionate, sharp-eyed comedy that grows in an unlikely garden . . . Nottage—better known for her serious-minded works such as *Ruined* and *Intimate Apparel*—knows her way around a punch line. It's not rim-shot comedy: Nottage gives these characters dimension and the pressure-valve humor grows organically."

—DOMINIC P. PAPATOLA, *PIONEER PRESS*

CLYDE'S

OTHER BOOKS BY LYNN NOTTAGE AVAILABLE FROM TCG

By the Way, Meet Vera Stark

Crumbs from the Table of Joy and Other Plays
ALSO INCLUDES:
Las Meninas
Mud, River, Stone
POOF!
Por'knockers

Intimate Apparel and *Fabulation*

Mlima's Tale

Ruined

Sweat

CLYDE'S

Lynn Nottage

THEATRE COMMUNICATIONS GROUP   NEW YORK   2024

Clyde's is published by Theatre Communications Group, Inc.,
520 Eighth Avenue, 20th Floor, Suite 2000, New York, NY 10018-4156

The publication of *Clyde's* by Lynn Nottage, through TCG Books, is made possible with support by Mellon Foundation.

Special thanks to Diane C. Yu for her generous support of this publication.

TCG books are exclusively distributed to the book trade by Consortium Book Sales and Distribution.

Library of Congress Control Numbers:
2023024286 (print) / 2023024287 (ebook)
ISBN 978-1-63670-000-7 (paperback) / ISBN 978-1-63670-018-2 (ebook)
A catalog record for this book is available from the Library of Congress.

Book design and composition by Lisa Govan
Cover design by Mark Melnick
Cover art compositing and retouching by Danielle Del Plato

First Edition, March 2024

In memory of Ron Cephas Jones

CLYDE'S

Following the death of George Floyd, the title of the play, which premiered in Minneapolis as *Floyd's*, was changed to *Clyde's*.

Floyd's had its world premiere at the Guthrie Theater (Joe Dowling and Joseph Haj, Artistic Directors) in Minneapolis on July 27, 2019. It was directed by Kate Whoriskey. The scenic design was by Lael Jellinek, the costume design was by Jennifer Moeller, the lighting design was by Christopher Akerlind, the sound design was by Justin Ellington, the original music was by Justin Hicks; the production stage manager was Tree O'Halloran. The cast was:

FLOYD	Johanna Day
MONTRELLOUS	John Earl Jelks
RAFAEL	Reza Salazar
LETITIA	Dame Jasmine Hughes
JASON	Andrew Veenstra

The Broadway premiere of *Clyde's* was produced by 2nd Stage (Carole Rothman, President and Artistic Director; Khady Kamara, Executive Director) at the Helen Hayes Theater on November 23, 2021. It was directed by Kate Whoriskey. The scenic design was by Takeshi Kata, the costume design was by Jennifer Moeller, the lighting design was by Christopher Akerlind, the sound design was by Justin Ellington, the original music was by Justin Hicks; the production stage manager was Donald Fried. The cast was:

CLYDE	Uzo Aduba
MONTRELLOUS	Ron Cephas Jones
RAFAEL	Reza Salazar
LETITIA	Kara Young
JASON	Edmund Donovan

SCENE 1

A truck stop sandwich shop. It sits on a nondescript stretch of road in Berks County, Pennsylvania, traveled by those looking for shortcuts, detours, or merely escape. It is a strange liminal space populated by folx down on their luck and looking for a second chance at life. Frequented by truckers and the occasional local, Clyde's, like many small businesses in postindustrial America, is trying hard to survive and carve out space in a rapidly evolving landscape. We are in the dingy kitchen, but it could be limbo. A sumptuous sandwich rests on the center of the counter. The zen-like Montrellous, forties, wise, talented, and cool as hell, meticulously garnishes a grilled cheese sandwich. He's the John Coltrane of sandwich making. It is all love for him, no drudgery involved in this process. He speaks as he works, never losing focus, though he's clearly wrapping up an elaborate and emotional story.

Clyde, forties, fierce and sexy, leans across the counter, intently listening, all steel, unmovable. The gravel in her voice betrays a life of cigarettes and whiskey, lived with gusto and no apology.

MONTRELLOUS: And . . . that was that. What else could I've done?

(Clyde lets out a long vocal exhale.)

Yeah.

CLYDE: God.

MONTRELLOUS: Yeah. Unfortunately, that's how it went down.

CLYDE: Well damn? How come you never told me that story?

MONTRELLOUS: I dunno.

CLYDE: So, like, why are you telling me this now? I mean, are you looking for sympathy? Or what? Cuz I'm sorry, I just don't.

MONTRELLOUS: I dunno. I thought you might be, um, moved.

CLYDE: Yeah? Well, you wanna know the last time I shed tears?

MONTRELLOUS: When?

CLYDE: Nevah. It's true. My mama used to stick me with her fingernail, kept it sharpened like a talon designed to inflict maximum pain, and every so often she'd poke me just to see if I'd cry. And you know how I reacted?

MONTRELLOUS: How?

CLYDE: Exactly as I'm reacting now.

(Clyde's face is devoid of any emotion.)

MONTRELLOUS: Yeah, but, were you really listening?

CLYDE: I was.

MONTRELLOUS: And?

CLYDE: Is there more you wanna say, or can I get on with my life?

MONTRELLOUS: That's it, that's your response?

CLYDE: Look, I'm not indifferent to suffering. But I don't do pity. I just don't. And you know why? Because . . . dudes like you thrive on it, it's your energy source, but like fossil fuels it creates pollution. That's why.

(Clyde laughs and lights a cigarette. She finds herself amusing.)

MONTRELLOUS: Well damn, apologies, it's only my life.

CLYDE: Whatevah. I did my time, you did your time. What the hell more do you want me to say?

MONTRELLOUS: I don't want you to say anything, I just want you to . . . try the sandwich.

(Montrellous cuts the grilled cheese sandwich in half, passes her the plate.)

(Sensually) Melted cheddar, garlic butter, on toasted sourdough bread, hand-baked . . . Try it.

CLYDE: I don't eat that FANCY crap.

MONTRELLOUS *(Seductively)*: Go on, expand yourself, it's better than that processed shit you force on e'rybody. Just taste it.

(Clyde eyes Montrellous and then the sandwich.)

CLYDE: Nah. I'm not hungry.

MONTRELLOUS: C'mon, one bite. It won't kill you.

CLYDE: Jesus Christ enough already.

(Montrellous pushes the sandwich a little closer to Clyde.)

Look, I've seen a million dudes like you. You get a little education inside, think you can buck the system, but you want my advice, don't strain yourself trying, you're too old for the rodeo.

MONTRELLOUS: It's going to be like that, huh? I don't need to know what kinda hustle you got going with those dudes from down south. But, I hear you got yourself in a little bit of . . . gambling debt.

CLYDE: Just keep the fuck out of it.

MONTRELLOUS: You don't need 'em. Really. You, me, a few tables, we can make this place do more than break even.

CLYDE: Excuse me, but you don't know the first thing about running a business, much less the sacrifices ya gotta make.

MONTRELLOUS: If that's what you wanna believe, but there's always a way out.

CLYDE: Ha! Don't fool yourself.

(A moment.)

MONTRELLOUS: You know, you're a beautiful woman. Don't sell yourself short.

CLYDE: Put the mojo back in your pants, Montrellous. Not interested.

MONTRELLOUS: Why can't you just receive a compliment without it being loaded? Why do you always wanna pick a fight?

CLYDE: Whatever game you are playing at, stop it. I'm not gonna do this little tango with you. I don't need a pimp.

MONTRELLOUS: Is that what you see?

(He eases the sandwich even closer to her, it appears to glow.)

Stay open.

(A moment. Clyde contemplates the sandwich.)

CLYDE: You know that story you just told me, if it was me, you know what I would've done in your situation?

MONTRELLOUS: No, what?

CLYDE: Walked the fuck away.

MONTRELLOUS: How could I?

CLYDE: Easy. Like this.

(As she leaves, Clyde extinguishes her cigarette in the sandwich, which spontaneously bursts into enormous flames.

Transition. Montrellous begins another sandwich—)

SCENE 2

Letitia, twenties, direct, self-possessed, and perhaps too quick to offer an opinion, and Rafael, twenties, a recovering addict who wears his emotions on his sleeve, watch as Montrellous, in master-chef mode, finishes the final touches on a sandwich.

It's a heightened moment. It should feel monumental, graceful, poetry-in-motion.

LETITIA: Listen up. My perfect sandwich? I got this. Peanut butter, grape jelly wit' a touch of cinnamon and nutmeg.

MONTRELLOUS and Rafael: Oooo.

RAFAEL: Cubano sandwich, with sour pickles, jalapeño aioli, and . . . and sweet onions.

LETITIA: Yo!

MONTRELLOUS: Nice.

(Rafael shoots Letitia a triumphant glance.)

LETITIA: Okay. What about a tuna melt, red onions, tomatoes . . . heirloom, romaine lettuce—

RAFAEL: Basic.

LETITIA: Wait, I ain't finished. Chopped lemongrass and basil on . . . a toasted black rye. There it is. Bam!

MONTRELLOUS: I feel it.

LETITIA: There you go!

RAFAEL: Hold up, I got it. Vietnamese sandwich, crisp baguette, barbecue pork—

MONTRELLOUS AND LETITIA: Mmm.

RAFAEL: Cilantro, diced sweet potatoes, a sprinkle of lime, and hold for it . . . horseradish.

(Letitia and Rafael high-five.)

LETITIA: Yes, goddamnit!

(Then, they turn their attention to Montrellous.)

Montrellous?

(He is suddenly a sensei.)

MONTRELLOUS: Maine lobster, potato roll gently toasted and buttered with roasted garlic, paprika, and cracked pepper with truffle mayo, caramelized fennel, and a sprinkle of . . . of . . . dill.

RAFAEL: Aw shit, you had to go there!

LETITIA: Stop it, my mouth just had a double orgasm.

(They all exhale. Bell rings.)

CLYDE *(Offstage)*: What the hell is going on in there? Anyone alive? Wakey. Wakey.

(We're back in a greasy kitchen. Everything looks ordinary. Clyde pops her head through the pass-through window.)

Where's my ham and cheese on white? *(Reverberating)* NOW!

(They are shocked back to reality. Then, Montrellous rings the bell.)

MONTRELLOUS: Ham and cheese on white.

(Transition.)

SCENE 3

Radio plays. Letitia does a fun, sexy dance, tightening an apron around her waist to accentuate her swaying hips and add a little style to her work ensemble. She wears a hairnet over her elaborate braids. Rafael gives playboy attitude, though his game is a little lame. He wears a red bandanna around his head.

Rafael meticulously salts chicken breasts, then turns them on the grill, salts the other side. Letitia preps a sandwich.

RAFAEL: Whatcha do last night? I rang you twice.

LETITIA: Never mind what I did, it was done.

RAFAEL: You missed out.

LETITIA: So it goes.

RAFAEL *(Flirtatiously)*: No really. You . . . missed . . . out!

LETITIA: Guess I did. But, I had real things to do.

RAFAEL: You gonna ask me what you missed?

LETITIA: Nope.

RAFAEL: A'ight. But, you missed . . . la celebración.

(Rafael does a show dance.)

LETITIA *(Flirtatiously)*: Okay. Whatevah.
RAFAEL: Your loss, mama. You're chasing ants, I can teach you
    to catch fireflies.
LETITIA: Guess what? Not interested.
RAFAEL: // Oh really?
LETITIA: So take my number out ya speed dial.

(A hand posts a new order.)

CLYDE *(Offstage)*: Look alive in there!

(Letitia rips down the order. Reads.)

LETITIA: Oh, c'mon. Really? What do that say?
RAFAEL: Lemme see. Damn, shit, dunno.

(Rafael attempts to decipher the order.)

That . . . Uh, that look like a C and a . . . J, so it gotta be
the fiery Cajun turkey wrap.

(Letitia sucks her teeth.)

LETITIA: Damn, that woman loves messing with us.

*(Letitia, frustrated, takes it out on the bread and turkey meat,
angrily preparing the sandwich.)*

RAFAEL: Oh my God.
LETITIA: What?!
RAFAEL: Slow down. Remember what Montrellous said 'bout
    preparing a sandwich. There's too much anger in your

fingers, girl. The sandwich is your pulpit, it's where you preach the gospel of good eating.

LETITIA: I know, I know he always be saying that, but I don't really get what he means. It's like bla bla bla. Sandwich. Whatevah.

(Letitia resets.)

RAFAEL: Relax. It's all about the process, mami.

(Letitia hurries through making the sandwich.)

LETITIA: Clyde don't have time for process. Nobody cares as long as it tastes right.

(A hand posts two more orders. Rafael rips them down and reads.)

RAFAEL: What? For real? Oh hell no.

LETITIA: What?

RAFAEL: The double bacon blue cheeseburger and cheesy bacon fries. Extra sauce. *(A string of Spanish expletives)* I feel like the fucking hangman. Why does Clyde keep this shit on the menu?

LETITIA: Monty be trying. You know, he still thinks we can turn this joke into a real spot.

RAFAEL: Yeah, right.

LETITIA: Like that joint on the hill that got that write-up in the *Sentinel*.

RAFAEL: It ain't gonna happen. Clyde launders money for some pendejo from down south.

LETITIA: You're lying.

RAFAEL: You seen them? They are from the underworld. Like seriously, el inframundo. I looked into this one dude's eyes, and it was like staring into the abyss.

LETITIA: The what?
RAFAEL: Abysssss.

(Rafael places chicken breasts in the fryer. They sizzle ominously.
Just then, Jason, late twenties, moody, white supremacist
tats on his face, enters tying his apron. Letitia and Rafael stop
what they're doing and stare.)

LETITIA: Who you? Where's Ronnie?
JASON: Who?
LETITIA: Ronnie Golmolka?
JASON: I dunno, was told to come back here by Clyde.
RAFAEL: Clyde?
JASON: Yeah.
LETITIA: Ain't nobody said shit to us. This is Ronnie's shift.
JASON: I don't know anything about that. But, Clyde said Ron-
nie was in violation. Got picked up. Possession. That's all
I heard.
LETITIA: Damn! When?
RAFAEL: Coño. Knew it. Told ya.
LETITIA: // Damn.

(They look at Jason.)

So, you know what you doing?
JASON: Yeah. Got trained over the weekend.
LETITIA: By who?!
JASON: Dunno, some guy who smells like patchouli and canola
oil.

(They always say Montrellous's name like he is a high holy man.)

LETITIA AND RAFAEL: Montrellous.
RAFAEL: Man, you're lucky.

JASON: So, where do I go?

LETITIA: Nowhere, as far as I'm concerned. We don't do that gang bullshit here.

JASON: Whatever. I'm not looking for trouble.

(Rafael stares at Jason, assessing.)

(To Rafael) What do you want? You the dishwasher?

RAFAEL: Do I look like the muthafucking dishwasher? I'm a sous-chef, bitch . . . but for now we're all just line cooks. The grill and fryer are mines. This is my territory, like the yard. Don't step across the line. Got it? Tish is on prep.

LETITIA: This mine.

(Letitia draws an air square around her area.)

JASON: Yeah, so what—

LETITIA: Golmolka, he also on prep. But, we all gotta do the sandwiches, cuz we're known for our sandwiches. But, when Montrellous is here—

RAFAEL AND LETITIA: We watch.

JASON: Yeah, I heard they got truckers drive miles outta their way for sandwiches.

RAFAEL AND LETITIA: Miles!

RAFAEL: None of us know what Montrellous does or how he does it, but all I know is you gotta respect it.

JASON: We're talking about a sandwich, right?

RAFAEL *(Snaps)*: Don't say that! When you taste his food you'll understand.

JASON: Understand what?

RAFAEL: Ohhh. That it ain't just about the sandwich.

LETITIA: Montrellous is a sensei. Drops garlic aioli like a realness bomb. He knows what we only wish to know.

JASON: What the fuck are you guys talking about?

RAFAEL (*Like a revelation*): A little salt makes the food taste good, too much salt makes the food inedible.

JASON: No shit.

RAFAEL: But, really think about it.

JASON: Okay, whatever. Just tell me where I stand.

RAFAEL: Over there. No. There. And dude, wash your fuckin' hands.

(*Jason washes his hands.*)

Hey you got a name?

JASON: Jason.

RAFAEL: I'm Rafael.

LETITIA: Letitia. But, people call me Tish.

JASON: Good to meet y'all.

LETITIA: We'll see about that.

RAFAEL: So . . . where you serve?

JASON: Upstate.

(*Letitia sizes him up.*)

LETITIA: Yeah. Shoulda guessed. You're one of them.

JASON: Nah, I'm just Jason. All right? Left the bullshit inside. I'm not looking to stir the pot. I wanna paycheck and peace.

LETITIA: That's what you all say. We'll see how long you last.

RAFAEL: I give you like three months, and you're back in.

LETITIA: Three? I give 'em two weeks. Haaaa!

JASON: Ain't gonna happen.

LETITIA: HmmMmm. Okay. Heard that before. Ask Golmolka, he was a haughty bitch like you.

(*Clyde pops up in the pass-through window armed with an order ticket, catching the crew off guard. Letitia and Jason both reach for the ticket, ending up in an uncomfortable proximity.*)

Sweetheart, we don't have time for socializing. We ain't on a date. Pans and utensils get scrapped and go in the machine. Ovah there. We move fast, so keep the fuck up. No time for breastfeeding or babysitting. You got it?

JASON: Yeah, I got it.

LETITIA: It's slow right now, but come dinnertime, when the truckers roll through, they been on the road, it's gonna get hella crazy.

RAFAEL: Hella crazy.

(Jason watches Letitia and Rafael assemble sandwiches.)

LETITIA: Whatcha waiting on? Let's see what you got.

RAFAEL: You know where to find everything, right?

JASON: Yeah.

LETITIA: You either step up or step out, cuz you ain't nobody here. So, ask if you don't know, cuz Clyde don't like mistakes. She don't play.

RAFAEL: She'll make you pay in blood.

LETITIA: Ain't nobody gonna hire us, and she knows it.

JASON: She seemed all right.

(Rafael and Letitia exchange a look.)

LETITIA: Just keep your head down. Cuz believe me, she'll make herself known. And then . . .

(Rafael places a completed sandwich in the window and rings the bell. Clyde instantly appears in the pass-through window. Rafael stiffens.)

CLYDE: Hello! Wakey wakey!

RAFAEL: Oh shit, you're up!

(Jason grabs the ticket.)

JASON: What the fuck does this say?
LETITIA: That's your first test. Good luck.

(Jason clumsily begins to make a sandwich. Transition.)

SCENE 4

Another day. Jason struggles through making a sandwich. It's a mess. He licks his fingers clean, then continues making the sandwich.
Letitia stares at Jason. Disbelief! Rafael silently flips burgers and chicken breasts on the grill.

LETITIA: Oh my God.

JASON: What?

LETITIA: Whatevah.

JASON: Is there something I can help you with?

LETITIA: I don't think so!

JASON: Something wrong? Every time I look up you're staring at me.

LETITIA: Well excuse me, if you don't wanna be looked at I suggest you make better cosmetic choices.

JASON: You know what?

LETITIA: What?

JASON: Fuck off.

LETITIA: Oooo. That language don't help, it's like hostile, and its implications made me feel, like, unvalidated. All right! I'm sensitive. And I don't have time for it.

JASON: Fuck off.

LETITIA: What's your problem?!

JASON: I don't have a problem.

LETITIA: Clearly you does.

JASON: I'm just trying to do my job. You're not gonna get into my head. Okay.

LETITIA: I didn't start this conversating.

JASON: You know what, can we make this a quiet space?

(Letitia sucks her teeth.)

. . .

(Letitia sucks her teeth again. They prep food in silence.)

LETITIA: So, what's up with them tats?

JASON: We talking again?

LETITIA: Hey Rafael, what was that dude's name? The one Clyde fired?

RAFAEL: Jeff Babbit.

(They have an opinion about Jeff, and it's not good.)

LETITIA: Yeah Jeff.

RAFAEL: Jeff.

LETITIA: JEFF-REY.

RAFAEL: Jeffrey.

LETITIA: He had to go—

RAFAEL: Cuz he was, like, this close to getting hurt.

LETITIA: He was a nasty one. Had them gang tats like yours. Liked to flex his "muscles." Stupid ass thought he was still in the prison yard. That shit don't fly 'round here.

JASON: You don't know anything about me.

LETITIA: That's what you think. I been around. I know all about breaking wild white horses.

JASON: Look. Good for you. I don't bother you, you don't bother me.

LETITIA: Well, you need to—

JASON: This is my lane, that's your lane. Can we like respect each other's lanes, keep moving, no talk—

LETITIA: I certainly don't need to talk to you, Mr. At-ti-tude . . . Mr. Ta-toos. Mr.—

JASON: Enough! Fucking hell. What's your problem?

LETITIA: Tone?! Tats! You started this conversating. I was like minding my own business. Thank you. I'm gonna be quiet, cuz I don't got nothing more to say to you.

JASON: Thank you! Can I focus on my food? Jesus!

LETITIA: And BTW, you need to shower.

JASON: That qualifies as talking.

LETITIA: Somebody needed to tell you. I'm done talking. Right, Rafael?

RAFAEL: A shower with soap. It's true. Don't be afraid to make soap your friend.

(Rafael and Letitia laugh.)

JASON: Ha, ha, ha. You guys done?

(A moment. They make sandwiches. Jason slaps a mess of pickles onto the sandwich, and then slathers it with creamy Parmesan dressing.)

LETITIA: Yo, yo, yo. Hold up. Hold up.

JASON: What now?!

LETITIA: You ain't doing that right. Why are you putting pickle relish on that sandwich? And so you know, you're not supposed to put that sauce on there. Is that the creamy Parmesan?

JASON: Yeah.

RAFAEL: Aw shit!

LETITIA: That's what I thought. You know, if somebody got hypertension, that sauce on that sandwich right there will kill 'em. Seriously!

RAFAEL: Homicide. Fourteen years to life. Right there, baby!

LETITIA: Cuz you know that's what happened to a guy—

RAFAEL: In August.

LETITIA: The bacon chili cheeseburger with—

RAFAEL: Extra pickles. // Died—

LETITIA: Died in the cab of his truck. Five bites. Salt. Fat. Bacon, chili, beef. Bam. Dead before 911 even got dialed. Hypertension. That's what they said. You want that shit on your conscience?

JASON: Who gives a fuck?

(Jason makes a show of wrapping the burger in wax paper.)

LETITIA: Clearly not you. Let it be, but it's gonna get sent back, cuz it ain't right. But, that's on you. I don't give a fuck. Hey Rafael, you give a fuck?

RAFAEL: Nah.

LETITIA: And you know how Clyde do when you don't get it right?

RAFAEL: She yell at you, and then she don't pay you.

LETITIA: Okay. See. But, you don't give a fuck! Whatever your name is. I'm not even gonna bother to ask you again, cuz I know you won't be here for but a minute.

(A moment. Rafael and Letitia make a show of watching Jason assemble the sandwich.)

Now you're just disrespectin' the lettuce.

JASON: Okay. You win. Tell me again, what am I supposed to put on it?

LETITIA: Oh now you want to know?

JASON: Yeah.

LETITIA: Is that the Manuel Luis Echegoyen La Fiesta Burger?

JASON: Yeah.

LETITIA: Three jalapeños, avocado, a tomato, lettuce—

RAFAEL: Cotija, onion, a dab of salsa verde and cilantro—

LETITIA: And, no fucking pickle relish!

(Jason remakes the sandwich. Letitia watches.)

That's it. Respect the recipe.

RAFAEL: There it is!

LETITIA: R-E-S-P-E-C-T!

RAFAEL: That sandwich was invented by Manuel Luis Echegoyen. It's one of our classics. // Yeah.

LETITIA: You want no problems, you stick with the recipe and Clyde won't give you no trouble. And believe me, you don't want trouble with that chick, cuz she's cray-cray.

RAFAEL: You'll see. Don't ask her nothing. Nada. And bro don't smile, cuz she don't like for nobody to be happy. Straight face. Don't even lift the corners of your mouth. Nothing!

LETITIA: Cuz if you're like me, you need this joint. You been out there, right?

JASON: Yeah.

LETITIA: You know what it's like. Ain't shit but misery. Seven months ago, I got out, that cold wind hit me hard, and things got real real. Seventy-five dollars in my pocket, nobody to hold my hand, nobody to say, "It's gonna be okay baby." I dialed the same number you dialed. And Clyde answered. And let me tell you something, you here cuz you done run outta options, ain't nobody gonna hire you except for Clyde. Especially you. The way you is. Cuz if you here, you done something. We all done something. And we just biding our time 'til we can get to another place.

RAFAEL: Straight up.

LETITIA: No, Clyde ain't nice, she may make ya crawl before ya walk. But, she knows the deal, she's the gatekeeper. And ain't no getting around it, so that muthafucking creamy Parmesan don't go on nothing but the Roma Mama chicken wrap. Comprende?

JASON: Yeah, I got it.

LETITIA: That's right.

(Jason finishes making the sandwich. Letitia rings the pick-up bell.

Transition.)

SCENE 5

Time has passed. Rafael works the grill and all of the prep stations alone. The tickets keep piling up. He's frantic. Rushing. Sweating.

It is a mad virtuosic dance to keep ahead of the tickets. Jason, hot and bothered, enters.

RAFAEL: Jesus, you're late. We're getting backed up. Quick, quick. Get on your apron.

JASON: Fucking Clyde.

RAFAEL: // Where you been?

JASON: I just asked for an advance to fill up my tank.

RAFAEL: C'mon, move it.

JASON: A simple request. And you know what she says? Walk. Walk. What's her deal?

RAFAEL: You gotta earn her trust. That's how she works, bro.

JASON: I mean, c'mon. I had to walk like eleven miles to get here. FUCKING BITCH!

(Jason puts on his apron.)

RAFAEL: Dude, don't even say that shit out loud, because I swear to God she can hear through walls. You call her bitch and she will eviscerate you.

(He makes gestures with knives.)

She don't play that sexist bullshit.

CLYDE *(Offstage)*: Jason!

RAFAEL: Oh shit.

CLYDE: *(Offstage)*: Jason!

RAFAEL: Oh no. You're in trouble now.

(Jason smiles.)

Don't smile. *(Whispers)* I'm serious, it makes her crazy.

(Clyde comes barreling in. She takes a sip of her beer, studying Jason and Rafael.)

(Whispers) Don't smile.

CLYDE: What the hell's going on? How come there's no food coming outta my kitchen? What's burning on the grill? Rafael?

RAFAEL: . . .

CLYDE: You!

JASON: . . .

CLYDE: You!

JASON: Yeah?

CLYDE: Jason.

JASON: Yeah.

CLYDE: Aggravated assault. Right?

JASON: Something like that.

CLYDE: So, you couldn't keep your hands to yourself? I hear you're a real tough one. See you were messing with that gang shit.

JASON: Not really.

CLYDE: You gonna make this work or what?

JASON: Yeah, whatever.

CLYDE: Cuz I'm talking doesn't mean you stop working.

JASON: Okay.

CLYDE: You want Rafael to run down the rules?

JASON: Nah. I got it.

CLYDE: He tell you what happens if I catch any of you morons stealing? Breaking my rules?

JASON: Yeah.

CLYDE: I don't go to the police. I deal with it my way. Understand?

JASON: I understand.

(Jason involuntarily smiles.)

CLYDE: Do you? Then what the hell are ya smiling at?

JASON: Nothing.

CLYDE: Oh, I'm nothing?!

(Clyde takes a sip of her beer.)

Don't look at me like you wanna fuck me. I bet you haven't seen pussy in a long time. That's right, I said it.

JASON: I'm not—

CLYDE: How long were you inside? Don't tell me you're not horny as a muthafucka.

JASON: Really?!

CLYDE: I'm playing with you. Ease up. You're cute. C'mon, I'm just playing with you.

(Clyde slaps Jason's ass.)

JASON: Don't they got laws about that kinda thing.

CLYDE: You gonna call the police?

(She slaps Jason on the ass again and grabs his butt cheeks.)

Oh c'mon, lighten up, I'm playing with you. And where's Tish? Huh?

(Clyde lights a cigarette.)

RAFAEL: Uh, she's, um, running late. She says she couldn't get help this afternoon.

CLYDE: She better not be bringing that kid in here again.

RAFAEL: She knows.

CLYDE: I love children, but hers is a frigging pinhead.

RAFAEL: That ain't cool, she's got adrenoleukodystrophy.

CLYDE: Boo-hoo. Like that's my problem. She shouldn't have smoked meth when she was pregnant.

RAFAEL: You know Tish don't do drugs.

CLYDE: Which side of the border are you on Rafael? Mine or hers?

(Jason smiles, he can't help it.)

RAFAEL: She's not bringing Carmen. I swear!

CLYDE: Look at you. You been working out Rafael? You finally taking testosterone? Sounds like you got a little more bass in your voice.

(Rafael can't quite muster the words.)

RAFAEL: . . .

CLYDE: I didn't hear ya?

(Jason smirks.)

What are you smiling at?

(Jason stops smirking.)

JASON: No, I was—

CLYDE: Don't wanna hear it. As far as I am concerned you don't need to talk unless you're answering a question. Just want food passed quickly through my window. Got it. So, why are you standing around like jackalopes wasting my time? C'mon! C'mon.

(Clyde claps her hands. They scramble back to work. Clyde watches them.

    Letitia rushes in tying her apron and putting on a head scarf. She washes her hands.)

Welcome. We're holding a spot for you to clean the fryer.

(Letitia groans.)

LETITIA: Sorry. You got my message?

CLYDE: Third time this month.

LETITIA: I know. I know. // I know.

CLYDE: What's going on?

LETITIA: My sitter fell through. It's hard to find good people since you switched up my hours. I need someone who can operate the medical equipment.

CLYDE: That's why I didn't have children, because I don't like excuses.

LETITIA: I know. I know. // Sorry.

CLYDE: Come see me later, Tish.

LETITIA: Clyde!

CLYDE: No discussion. And what are you wearing on your head? That ain't regulation.

LETITIA: C'mon Clyde, I just got my hair did.

CLYDE: Really? Well, sweetheart, I recommend you get your money back.

(Clyde leaves. A long loud collective exhale.)

JASON: Thank God.

RAFAEL: I didn't think I could hold my breath that long.

JASON: She's like a little horny dude.

RAFAEL: Yup. And she'll also give you a beating like one. She kicked my ass last week.

JASON: Shut up!

RAFAEL: Hell yeah.

(Rafael holds up his shirt to reveal a large bruise.)

JASON: Holy shit!

RAFAEL: Yup! I know. She don't look it, but she's strong as hell. Got, like, Lucha Libre moves.

JASON: Are you serious?

RAFAEL: Bro, it's real. Do not cross her. She'll make you suffer.

JASON: Shit, what's up with her?

(Rafael checks the window, before—)

RAFAEL: Yeah, she's like a licensed dominatrix.

JASON: Whoa.

LETITIA: She did time, yup. That's why she hires us.

JASON: What she do?

LETITIA: I heard her husband changed the safe word, but she couldn't remember it.

(Letitia wraps her hands around her neck, as if choking.)

JASON: Get the fuck outta here.

(Letitia returns to work, agitated.)

RAFAEL: Hey, mami, you okay?

LETITIA: No. I had to leave Carmen with my ex.

RAFAEL: I thought—

LETITIA: But, what else I'm supposed to do? I couldn't find anybody who knows how to care for her properly.

RAFAEL: I thought the court said you wasn't supposed to leave her with him.

LETITIA: I'm not. But—

RAFAEL: If you need help, I told you call mi hermana, give her a few dollars and she'll watch Carmen—

LETITIA: Now you got me worried. You got your cell on you?

RAFAEL: Here.

(Rafael passes her the cell.)

Don't use up all my minutes.

(Letitia dials.)

LETITIA: C'mon, Keith. C'mon. Why ain't you picking up? Voicemail.

(Letitia dials again. Nothing.)

Goddamnit.

RAFAEL: I'm sure it's okay. Maybe he took her out.

LETITIA: Shit.

RAFAEL: Don't worry. He's not going to let anything happen to her.

LETITIA: He better not be getting high.

RAFAEL: He smokes some weed. What's the worst thing that happens, he turns on the television, falls asleep, and lets the TV do the babysitting. C'mon. Clyde's in her mood. So, get going, before she comes back in here and squeezes my nuts.

(Letitia puts on her apron.)

JASON: You okay?
LETITIA: Don't talk to me. Just pass me a ticket.

(Jason passes her the ticket.)

JASON: Hey, Tish.
LETITIA: No, // I'm not in the mood!
RAFAEL: Don't. Not now.
JASON: I was just gonna say—
LETITIA: Look, I don't need advice from a hater like you.
JASON: I'm not a hater.
LETITIA: So, the racist tats were just an accident.
JASON: No, but—
LETITIA: That's what I'm gonna call you. No butt.

(Rafael laughs.)

JASON: Ha ha ha. You guys are fucking idiots.
RAFAEL: Hey. Quick. Check the door.
LETITIA: All clear.

(Rafael takes a sandwich out of the refrigerator.)

JASON: Hey, what's up?

(Rafael proudly displays the sandwich.)

RAFAEL: I've designed a sandwich. Try it.

(Letitia takes a bite, Rafael watches. She considers.)

LETITIA: Nope.
RAFAEL: Fuck. Almost?!
LETITIA: Not quite. Too salty.
RAFAEL: Damn. You try it.
JASON: Why?
RAFAEL: I been working on somethin' special. Montrellous say the first bite should be an invitation that you can't refuse, and if you get it right, it'll transport you to another place, a memory, a desire cuz like everything he touches be sublime.
JASON: What's that mean?
RAFAEL: Like beyond amazing, like how is it possible? And both of us are working on it, cuz like cuz, you know.

(Jason takes a bite of the sandwich.)

JASON: It's good.
RAFAEL: It's good, but is it great?
JASON: I dunno, I mean it's a turkey sandwich.
RAFAEL *(Devastated)*: Fuck!

(Rafael grabs the sandwich and throws it in the garbage.)

LETITIA: You'll get there.

(They work in silence. Orders appear in the window. Transition.)

SCENE 6

Jason, Rafael and Letitia watch Montrellous making a sandwich.

RAFAEL: Baby eggplant parmigiana with black olives, capers, and anchovies, what's that sauce called?

MONTRELLOUS: Puttanesca.

RAFAEL: Yeah. Puttanesca on an olive and rosemary ciabatta.

LETITIA: Damn!

RAFAEL: Yup.

MONTRELLOUS: Dig it.

LETITIA: Okay. Bacon, lettuce, and . . . grilled squash on cornbread wit' molasses butter.

RAFAEL: Molasses butter?

LETITIA: Molasses butter, nigga. Dream.

JASON: I got one. A Philly Swiss cheesesteak on . . . wheat.

(A moment.)

LETITIA: Seriously? We're all bringin' our A game, and you're talking about a Philly cheesesteak on weak.

MONTRELLOUS: I love a Philly cheesesteak.

LETITIA: What?

JASON: Ba-Bam!

LETITIA: Whatevah . . . Montrellous.

MONTRELLOUS: Curried quail egg salad with mint on oven-fresh cranberry pecan multigrain bread.

ALL: Mmm. Ahhh.

(Bell rings. Abruptly interrupting the moment. They're back. Clyde stands in the doorway.)

CLYDE: What's going on in here? Where's my tuna on rye?

(Montrellous rings the bell.)

MONTRELLOUS: Tuna on rye.

(Transition.)

SCENE 7

Clyde enters with supplies as Jason, Rafael and Letitia work around her. She is clearly in the way and enjoying being an obstacle to their work.

CLYDE: Look alive! We got twenty Genoa salamis. All right, Kobe beef. Two boxes of virgin olive oil from Serbia! Don't know where that is, but sounds like some good shit. So, don't say I don't do anything for you.

JASON: Where'd all this come from? Is this stuff legal?

CLYDE: When were you authorized to ask questions? Just open it.

(She kicks the box over to Jason. He opens it.)

Huh? What's this?

(Reading the label.)

"Swiss chard."

LETITIA: What's that?

CLYDE: The hell if I know.

LETITIA: What are we supposed to do with it?

CLYDE: Figure it out. You're welcome. Playtime is over. I'm losing money. Don't gimme that look, if you don't like the way I run things, you're welcome to leave, but good luck with that.

(Clyde laughs and finally leaves.)

RAFAEL: Hijo de puta. How the fuck did we get stuck here?

JASON: Tell me about it.

RAFAEL: You know I tried for like two months to get another gig, and Clyde's the only person who would even look me in the eye.

LETITIA: Yup! Real talk!

JASON: Dude, why were you locked up?

RAFAEL: I held up a bank.

JASON: No shit.

RAFAEL: Yeah.

LETITIA: That's gangsta, right.

RAFAEL: If only.

JASON: How long you serve?

RAFAEL: Too long.

JASON: Where they have you?

RAFAEL: Frackville.

JASON: No way.

RAFAEL: Yeah. I was strung out, thought I could withdraw money from Wells Fargo with my nephew's BB gun. I don't know what I was thinking. Downtown. Six days before Christmas. I was like outta my head with love. I had all these big muthafucking plans. I was gonna buy my girl a dog, but not like any dog, it cost like fifteen hundred dollars.

JASON: Why didn't you just go to the pound?

RAFAEL: It was like a pure breed. A Cavalier King Charles Spaniel, bitch. You can't get that at no pound. So, middle of the day, I go into the bank, pull out my gun, and I say shit like from the movies. "Everyone put your hands up, this is a robbery!" I was so high, bro, I shot one of the security guards in the mouth with the BB, that got me like an extra year for assault. The BB like cracked his tooth and got caught in the back of his throat and he started to choke. And I had to like do the muthafuckin' Heimlich on this dude. And then the police was on me so fast, I didn't have time to blink. It was like "blink!" I'm cuffed and a felon. That shit's true.

JASON: Not true!

RAFAEL: True. I'm a romantic. I love with every part of my body. What can I tell you, dope makes you do dumb-ass shit.

JASON (*Jokingly*): So, you know where I can get some?

RAFAEL: Shut up. Don't wanna hear it. I'm totally clean. Sober. There it is baby!

(*Rafael takes out his medallion, kisses it and then shows it to Jason. Rafael's cell phone rings. He answers.*)

No, who's this? You called me. I didn't call you. No, I didn't call you muthafucka—

LETITIA: Is that Keith? Gimme the phone.

(*Letitia grabs the phone.*)

(*On phone*) Keith! How come you didn't answer? Just answer when I call you, I don't care if you don't recognize the number. Rafael! No, he's not my man. // No, I said he's not my man.

RAFAEL: I could be.

LETITIA *(On phone)*: What if it was an emergency? Well, it could have been. Yes. Yes. NO! I just wanted to make sure that you feed Carmen. Just feed her! I don't need to know that. No McDonald's bullshit this time. Real food. Fruit. Vegetables. Goodbye.

(Letitia hands Rafael back his phone.)

Oh my God. He's soooo stupid.

RAFAEL: Everything okay?

LETITIA: Yeah. Thanks, Rafael.

RAFAEL: You know, this wouldn't happen if you had somebody to—

LETITIA: No // no.

RAFAEL: Your mistake. I can give you excellent references. Satisfaction guaranteed.

LETITIA: Very funny.

RAFAEL: And sexy?

(Letitia smiles.)

LETITIA: A lil bit. Watch the grill.

RAFAEL: I'm just putting it out there.

LETITIA: Well, put it back in there. Cuz, I really don't need to see it.

(Jason laughs.)

He laughs.

JASON: . . .

(A moment. Seriousness descends.)

LETITIA: Yo, I hope Keith don't—

RAFAEL: I'm playing, but it'll be okay.

LETITIA: Thanks.

(Rafael seizes the moment to give Letitia a warm hug.)

JASON: This is making me very uncomfortable.

LETITIA: Okay. That's enou—

RAFAEL: Hmm. I like the extra weight.

LETITIA: Get outta here! You wouldn't even know what to do with all of this.

(Letitia playfully pulls away.)

JASON: You guys make me laugh.

(Jason smiles.)

LETITIA: Well, we're not here for your entertainment.

JASON: I know. I'm just saying.

RAFAEL: It's about time you said somethin'.

JASON: I'm not a big talker.

RAFAEL: Yeah, that's kinda clear.

JASON: I just, umm, ain't had many folks to talk to since I got out.

RAFAEL: You ain't really said what you done.

JASON: I told ya, assault.

RAFAEL: But, your tats tell another story.

JASON: Tats tell you I was trying to survive, that's all. They don't mean shit.

LETITIA: You inked up when it was convenient, and now it don't mean nothing when it ain't. I look atchu, and I know one thing, wearing that much hate's gonna drag you down. And you seem all right.

JASON: I don't wanna talk about it.

RAFAEL: That's not how it works here. It's kind of a ritual, we speak the truth. Then, let go and cook. Montrellous taught us that. We leave the pain in the pan. We got each other's backs, that's how we get back up.

JASON: Bullshit! C'mon. Have you looked around? This place is a dump.

LETITIA: Seriously. I broke into the pharmacy to cop seizure medication for my daughter. Didn't have no insurance. They kept turning me down, and Carmen woulda died before all of the Medicaid paperwork went through. It was expensive, and I was panicked, you know, got desperate, not thinkin'. That's the truth of it. I would've done anythin' to protect her. I would fuckin' do it again. But my mistake, and this is on me, I got greedy while I was in the pharmacy, and took me some oxy and addy to sell on the side. And . . . I got caught. Simple as that.

JASON: . . . I hurt a couple people. Real bad. Let my anger get ahead of me. That's it. Did my time.

RAFAEL: Okay. You don't have tell us everythin' now. But, don't that feel better?

LETITIA: C'mon. Let's show Clyde what we got.

(They return to cooking. Transition.)

SCENE 8

Montrellous meticulously prepares a sandwich. Rafael, Jason and Letitia watch. The symphony.
    Montrellous cuts the sandwich into four sections.

MONTRELLOUS: Take in that aroma. What do you smell?

    (Montrellous passes around a sprig of thyme and a chili pepper. They each take a turn smelling it.)

    That thyme is from the garden that I planted out back this spring. A lil bit of sunshine and rainwater and there you go. Look at that color. Dope, right?

RAFAEL: Damn!

MONTRELLOUS: It took two months to grow. From the soil, to my hand, to a stranger's mouth where it will awaken a new sensation. Try it. C'mon, quickly, quickly, before Clyde docks our pay.

(They each take a section of the sandwich. Bite in. Ecstasy.)

JASON: What the hell?!

RAFAEL: Seriously?! // Unbelievable.

LETITIA: Damn, I don't understand what I'm eating? It's like, like heaven.

MONTRELLOUS: Yeah. I've been experimenting with that sandwich. Simplicity. New flavor profiles. I baked the bread myself. Herb focaccia.

RAFAEL: What is this?

MONTRELLOUS: Grilled Halloumi.

JASON: THIS is everything!

MONTRELLOUS: Beautiful. I'm glad you dig it. You know why I love the sandwich, cuz it's a complete meal that you can hold between your fingers. It's the most democratic of all foods. Two pieces of bread, and between, you can put anything you want. It invites invention and collaboration.

RAFAEL: Jesus, I make a sandwich every day, but somehow your shit always tastes like the truth.

MONTRELLOUS: It's about order, baby. I'm interested in the composition, it's not merely about flavor. Dig? I think about the balance of ingredients and the journey I want the consumer to take with each bite. Then, finally, how I can achieve oneness with the sandwich.

LETITIA: I've been trying to do what you say, but—

MONTRELLOUS: It's because you bring all the chaos from home into this kitchen.

LETITIA: I try not to.

MONTRELLOUS: Let it go for two minutes, Tish. Be here and nowhere else. Let whatever you're feeling become part of your process, not an impediment.

LETITIA: I'm like trying, but I can't shake what's out there. I'm supporting all of them on this gig. And everybody wants something that I can't give 'em. And my baby's daddy is like hittin' me up for money and pressuring me to move back in.

MONTRELLOUS: I hear you. But, think about your daughter, what if you could create something perfect for her? Something that reflects your love. What if you took the few minutes it takes to really prepare that sandwich? What if you decided to say with every drop of your special sauce, "I love you, Carmen." What if this sandwich represented your love. Think about it. When I made that sandwich, you know what I was thinking?

LETITIA: No, what?

MONTRELLOUS: This sandwich is my strength. This sandwich is my victory. This sandwich is my freedom.

(Tears well up in Letitia's eyes. She cries.)

LETITIA: I'm trying.

MONTRELLOUS: And what I find is that you gotta surprise yourself with an ingredient that shouldn't work, something that pulls it all together. Think about that challenging flavor that's gonna defy expectation, and elevate your sandwich, even if the mouth tasting it doesn't receive it that way.

LETITIA: Yeah. I hear you.

MONTRELLOUS: You know, I've tried to share this with Clyde, you know, get her in the kitchen to feel the ingredients between her fingers. Make her see that this sandwich is the culmination of a long hard journey that began with a wheat seed cultivated by a farmer thousands of years ago.

JASON *(A revelation)*: Whoa!

MONTRELLOUS: Have another bite.

(Jason bites into the sandwich.)

JASON: Can you show me how to make that sandwich?

MONTRELLOUS: I can show you how to make it, but balance is as important as imbalance. Where my hand leads, may not be where your hand takes you. It's the intangible grace of flavors and aromas that tell your story, and that's only achieved through practice.

JASON: What if I can't do it?

MONTRELLOUS: You can.

RAFAEL: Man, don't sweat it, I've been trying for almost eight months to capture somethin' like that joint right there. But, I don't get it. I just don't fucking get it.

MONTRELLOUS: You will.

RAFAEL: And if I don't.

MONTRELLOUS: All you can do is control the intention. You'll get there, baby.

JASON: Are you this smooth all the time? Cuz your lady must, like, love you.

MONTRELLOUS: She does.

LETITIA: Yo, hold up, Monty, I didn't know you had a lady.

MONTRELLOUS: Yeah.

RAFAEL: Yeah?

MONTRELLOUS: Vanessa.

LETITIA: Where have you been hiding Ms. Vanessa? How come we don't know about her?

MONTRELLOUS: Now you do.

RAFAEL: I bet she's fine.

MONTRELLOUS: Let me tell you something about Vanessa. She's the most unassuming woman you'll ever meet, but when I'm with her I feel absolutely at peace, and that's worth gold. You know why?

LETITIA: Nah.

MONTRELLOUS: Cuz I got off the Bieber bus with seven tens and a five-dollar bill in my pocket, a toothbrush, and the clothing on my back. And it wasn't even my own clothing, it was given to me by the prison system. They dropped me on that street, and there was nobody I could call to come get me. So, I went to this real nice restaurant, had me a good hot meal, two glasses of pinot noir, then spent half the night in the bus station pretending like I was waiting on somebody to come. At about seven A.M. the next morning, I realized I was about outta money and options, and then Vanessa walked in. I can't remember where she was going, but she said good morning to me in a way that brought me back to life. Her greeting was filled with the kinda optimism you encounter so . . . infrequently. And the fact that Nessa, this unadorned woman, wanted my meager offerings, reassured me.

RAFAEL: Damn, leave it to Montrellous to make me want an ugly woman.

MONTRELLOUS: There's nothing ugly about Vanessa. Let's be clear about that. She's a beautiful woman.

LETITIA: That's so nice, Monty. I didn't know.

MONTRELLOUS: Now you do.

RAFAEL: You're full of surprises.

MONTRELLOUS: I give myself a surprise every day, sometimes it's as simple as cooking for my lady or picking up an imperfect pebble. And now, I'm taking a break and a smoke. If Clyde comes in, offer her the last bite of that sandwich.

(Montrellous leaves.)

RAFAEL: Yo, he just took my break.

LETITIA: That was some shaman shit right there!

JASON: Psst. Why'd Montrellous do time?

LETITIA: Nobody knows.

RAFAEL: Well, I heard that he went to prison on principle. It was like an act of rebellion. He willfully chose to confront the evil, infiltrate and undermine the prison-industrial complex from the inside.

JASON: That sounds like grade-A bullshit.

RAFAEL: Most us get caught in the web of destruction, Montrellous met the evil head-on. He never succumbed to the things that generally pull us down, so that when he was there, he could fight the system with all of his muscle.

JASON: Dude, you lost me.

RAFAEL: It's some deep and confusing shit, but realness on a level that I find perplexing and heroic.

JASON: Maybe, he's just like crazy. You ever thought about that?

RAFAEL: Nah, he ain't crazy. Montrellous, he like the Buddha if he'd grown up in the hood. There's so much to learn and absorb that I feel small in his presence. I WAS a total nonbeliever at first, the prince of all haters. I resisted the knowledge, fought like a gangbanger, and allowed doubt to cloud my faith, but then I tasted his pastrami on rye. Madre mía. He makes believers out of even the most jaded vegans.

JASON: I give him that. He can make a mean-ass sandwich.

LETITIA: There you go!

CLYDE (*Suspiciously, from window*): Are you all on a break or what?

(*She pops her head in the window, but disappears as quickly as she appeared. Letitia bristles.*)

LETITIA: But, tell that shit to Clyde, that woman refuses to open her heart to anything good.

RAFAEL: Yo. This dude who worked the register, he tol' me she sold her soul to get this joint.

JASON: C'mon.

RAFAEL: Be careful. Have you ever seen her eat? I'm just saying.

(Rafael gives him a look that says, "I ain't lying."
Clyde appears, as if miraculously.)

CLYDE: Why is it so damn quiet in here? Where's Montrellous?

(Jason views her with new eyes.)

LETITIA: Out back, but he saved a little bit of sandwich for you.

(The sandwich is illuminated, it tempts and calls to Clyde. She
resists the glow.)

CLYDE: . . . Not interested.
RAFAEL: One bite.
JASON: It's delicious.

(Once again the sandwich is illuminated, it tempts and calls to
Clyde. She resists.)

CLYDE: No . . . no . . . no. I have acid reflux.
JASON: Yeah, right.
CLYDE: Excuse me, what did you say?

(Clyde walks over to Jason and gets into his personal space.)

JASON: What?
CLYDE: I asked you what you said?
JASON: Uh, I didn't—
CLYDE: I like a man of a few words. Your parole officer, what
was his name again?
JASON: Evan.
CLYDE: You want me to call Evan, and tell him how you tried
to touch my ass?
JASON: But, I didn't.

CLYDE: Well, somehow. I feel like you did. I feel compromised. You all saw it, right?

(A moment.)

You saw it, Tish.

(Letitia looks away.)

JASON: Maybe if you had somebody, you wouldn't be so damn hard on us.

CLYDE: What makes you think I don't have somebody?

LETITIA: Yo Clyde, do you know a chick named Vanessa?

CLYDE: No. Who's she?

LETITIA: Monty's lady.

(Clyde tries not to be bothered by this information. Letitia laughs.)

CLYDE: Vanessa! Well, good for Monty, but he ain't exactly the valentine I'd want.

LETITIA: Well, I don't know about you, but me, personally, I want a dude like Monty, yup, someone who'll take me to dinner, like a nice place, and while we was eating, he'd give me a box of chocolates, flowers, and one of those stuffed animals with a heart. Because I like something soft, even if it's a little corny. Then we'd do something special like go to the movies or roller-skating, and he would take me home, not expecting nothing but one kiss and a thank-you.

JASON: Don't hold your breath. You might get flowers and dinner, but the other stuff. That's asking too much. And what does the guy get in return?

LETITIA: A kiss. Okaaay.

JASON *(Playfully)*: That doesn't seem like a fair deal.

LETITIA: And when was the last time you went out on a date?

JASON: Like a date date?

LETITIA: Yeah.

JASON: You mean like, a date? That's not what I do.

LETITIA: Why doesn't that surprise me?

JASON: The women I date don't need all of that nonsense.

LETITIA: Everybody needs all of that. Right Clyde?

CLYDE *(Casually)*: Here's the deal, if a man goes through the trouble of buying you flowers, chocolates, dinner, and a movie, believe me he ain't gonna be satisfied with a kiss at the end of the evening. He wants to bend you over and fuck you in the ass. That's the thank-you he's looking for. Men don't go through all that trouble for a kiss. Am I lying, guys?

(Jason and Rafael avoid Clyde's eyes.)

LETITIA: Well, I'm looking for the man that does.

CLYDE: Good luck with that babycakes. When was the last time a man bought you flowers and didn't ask you for a blow job? I'm just saying.

(This hurts Letitia.)

LETITIA: Who the hell hurt you?

CLYDE: What makes you think I was the one that got hurt? Last man that tried isn't around to try again, I made damn sure of that. Did my time without regrets. *(Imitating Letitia)* Okaaay.

LETITIA: I can't!

(Letitia holds up her hand and returns her hyperfocus to making sandwiches. Montrellous reenters. Clyde responds to Letitia, but her words are for Montrellous.)

CLYDE: And Tish, my advice. Set your sights higher. You know what kinda guy impresses me? The kind with a two-car garage, a house with central air, and a full-time job. If he has all of that, I don't care if he wants to take me to dinner at Taco Bell and only gets me a gift once a year at Christmastime. If a guy needs all that fancy window dressing then, trust me, he's hiding something. But, what do I know?

JASON: When was the last time you went on a date?

CLYDE: Yesterday!

JASON: Really?!

CLYDE: Yeah! And you wanna know what we did?

(Clyde makes a provocative sexual gesture.)

JASON: No!

(Clyde laughs.)

MONTRELLOUS: Well, I hope they're good people and treat you right.

(This catches Clyde off guard.)

CLYDE: They do.

MONTRELLOUS: That's beautiful, you are a dynamic woman, and should know what it's like to be treated with love. Kindness.

CLYDE: That smooth buttery bullshit don't fly with me.

(Clyde looks at Montrellous, then to his sandwich.)

MONTRELLOUS: One bite left.

CLYDE: Yeah? What's in it?

MONTRELLOUS: I've been experimenting with some new combinations.

CLYDE: Better not be on my time.

MONTRELLOUS: Go on, take a bite. Tell me what you think.

CLYDE: Do I look hungry?

MONTRELLOUS *(Seductively)*: C'mon. Don't you remember when your mother cooked you something special, even if it was only a can of Campbell's soup heated to perfection. And you said I'm not hungry, and she made you eat it, and you tasted the warm broth, and it made you feel . . . happy, loved.

CLYDE *(A flash of vulnerability)*: My mother never cooked anything. Cereal and a frozen pizza if we were lucky. That woman was like peanut brittle, sweet and salty, and I was never sure whether I actually liked her. So don't try that shit with me.

MONTRELLOUS: Go on. One bite.

(A moment.)

CLYDE: Maybe . . .

(Clyde picks up the sandwich. Everyone is excited, could this finally be the moment.

Or maybe not. Clyde tosses the sandwich into the garbage. A collective gasp.)

LETITIA: Noooo!

JASON: Damn, I woulda eaten that.

CLYDE: All that inspiration he's been feeding you rejects, you see where it ended up. If I catch you stealing my food again, I'll make sure each and every one of ya pay. Am I clear?

(Clyde stares them down and leaves. Collective exhale.)

RAFAEL: I don't know why she scares me. I mean I've battled some bad demons, but—

JASON: I know. Shit. Look at my hand.

(Jason's hand quivers.)

She actually might be the devil.

LETITIA: If she was a dude, none of y'all would have a problem. You got no idea what it's like for us out here. If she hard, believe me, that bitch probably earned that shit.

MONTRELLOUS: True that. Being incarcerated took a little something from all of us . . . including Clyde.

JASON: That's for damn sure.

MONTRELLOUS: And you know what they say, cuz you left prison don't mean you outta prison. But, remember, everything we do here is to escape that mentality. This kitchen, these ingredients, these are our tools. We have what we need. So, let's cook.

(They all pick up knives and dive into prep work. Transition.)

SCENE 9

Rafael stands guard at the pass-through window.

RAFAEL: We're good.
LETITIA: You sure?
RAFAEL: C'mon. Quickly.

> *(Letitia nervously presents a sandwich to Rafael and Jason. Montrellous examines the sandwich, then tastes it.)*

LETITIA: And?
MONTRELLOUS: Not bad.
LETITIA: But not good?
MONTRELLOUS: It's . . . not bad.
LETITIA: Damn! I thought I was close. What about my special sauce?
MONTRELLOUS: I can taste your impatience.
LETITIA: Forget it!

(Letitia tosses the sandwich into the garbage.)

MONTRELLOUS: Hey!

LETITIA: It's just a fucking sandwich, who gives a shit?!

RAFAEL: I liked it.

LETITIA: Who cares?

RAFAEL: I thought it was good.

LETITIA: I'm sorry. I'm not gonna get there. And Montrellous, don't tell me I will. Just stop.

(Letitia can't fight back the emotions. Tears.)

MONTRELLOUS: Hey. Hey. Don't give up. You know, cooking—

LETITIA: I don't want to hear it. It's like, I can't!

MONTRELLOUS: Okay.

LETITIA: I mean, I'm like no further along than I was six months ago. I'm gonna be thirty on Friday, and I can't even make a sandwich taste right. Yesterday, I caught my daughter staring at me, and I kept thinking what does she see when she looks at me? This woman who can't even hold it together.

RAFAEL: We all got them days.

LETITIA: But, it's like every day.

(Bell rings.

Montrellous takes the slip and begins to prepare a sandwich as he speaks. Frustrated, Letitia butchers a head of lettuce.)

MONTRELLOUS: A couple months after I got out, I sank into a very dark place. I couldn't see beyond my depression. I couldn't bear it. And then one day I walked into the supermarket, and I saw this absolutely perfect artichoke. It was beautiful. Green. Symmetrical. A grace note. And I needed to have it. And when I got home I stared at it for a long time, then realized I didn't know what the hell to do with an artichoke. So, I went online, found a recipe. The five easy steps to preparing an artichoke.

(Montrellous takes the knife from Letitia's hand.)

And I began to clip the petals. Soaked 'em in lemon water. Steamed 'em, then ate it. And I realized there must be other things in the produce section that I've never tasted. And the next day I went back, and soon I found that going to the supermarket gave me this . . . renewed sense of purpose, I wanted to find the most perfect things to combine to make something delicious. I could spend an hour studying the produce, smelling it, feeling it, thinking about its journey, all the hands that touched it. And then I'd go home and prepare a meal for myself and my lady, that made me happy. And slowly those meals for us resurrected my spirit. It awakened something. Until then, I thought I needed more to give me joy, to complete me. And right then, I understood that the most essential thing, sustenance, was enough to make me content. Here.

(Montrellous hands the knife to Letitia.)

Do you want to help me?

(Montrellous slows Letitia's hands, she gets into a more even and relaxed rhythm of cutting.)

LETITIA: Thank you.
RAFAEL: Hey Tish. I know Friday's your birthday, and if you ain't doing nothing, I'd like to help you celebrate.
LETITIA: I dunno.
RAFAEL: Why not?

LETITIA: Cuz.

RAFAEL: Cuz, you ain't got nothing to wear.

LETITIA: I got stuff to wear.

RAFAEL: Then what?

LETITIA: . . .

RAFAEL: I will turn it out. You ain't seen me on a Friday night.

LETITIA: I can imagine.

RAFAEL: I don't think you got that much imagination, mami, otherwise you already woulda said yes.

LETITIA: Oh, please.

RAFAEL: Why not?

LETITIA: Okay . . . Maybe.

RAFAEL: I can work with maybe. You won't regret it!

(Transition.)

SCENE 10

Clyde, cigarette in her mouth, enters with two bags of rancid sea bass as Letitia and Rafael prepare food.

CLYDE: Don't thank me! But guess who got you fifteen pounds of Chilean sea bass! Got a good deal, and didn't even have to fuck anybody.

RAFAEL: The fish smells rank.

CLYDE: You know my policy. If it ain't brown or gray it can be fried.

RAFAEL: You sure?

CLYDE: Give it here. Let me smell it.

(Rafael passes a piece of fish to Clyde. She takes a whiff, fights back an involuntary gag.)

Oh shit.

(She collects herself.)

It's okay.

RAFAEL: You sure?

CLYDE: How many times are you gonna ask? Did I vomit?

RAFAEL: No.

CLYDE: Then, it's fine.

RAFAEL: Okaaay.

(Rafael and Letitia exchange looks.)

CLYDE: Don't gimme that look. This is how business works. You think guys on Wall Street don't cut corners? You think Colonel fucking Sanders didn't fry up a couple of rats to make ends meet? And don't tell me you two don't break rules. Cuz—

LETITIA: Whatevah. But, what if somebody get sick?

CLYDE: So what? They get a touch of diarrhea. They go home, spend a night on the toilet and next time they come in, they'll get a free beer. Problem solved.

LETITIA *(Dubious)*: Okaaay.

(Rafael examines the fish, then places it in the refrigerator. Jason enters.)

JASON: Hey, sorry.

CLYDE: Oh, welcome. You need a coffee, sweetheart? You wanna take a moment?

JASON: Sure, that would be great.

CLYDE: Get the fuck outta here, where have you been?

JASON: I'm here!

CLYDE: We don't do late . . . here.

JASON: I know. I got it.

(A moment.)

CLYDE: You okay?

JASON: Yeah. Just, you know—

CLYDE *(Softening)*: Look, sometimes I give you guys a hard time, but if you need help my door is always open.

JASON *(Sincerely)*: Thanks, Clyde. I appreciate it.

CLYDE: Yeah, you like that? Fuck you, I don't give a shit, just get here on time.

(Clyde turns to leave. Jason puts on his apron and washes his hands.)

JASON: Why you always gotta be that way? // What did we do to you?

LETITIA: I wouldn't.

CLYDE: It's not what you did to me, it's what you did to yourself. You ain't happy here?

JASON: . . .

CLYDE: I'm asking you a question?

JASON: . . .

LETITIA: Yo, Clyde—

CLYDE: I suggest you stay out of this. *(To Jason)* I asked you a question.

JASON: You know I need this job.

CLYDE: Yeah, that's right. So—

JASON: I just don't get why you always gotta . . .

CLYDE: What?

JASON: Be so hard on us. You of all people know how tough it is to get out. You know what we face down every day. I mean, fucking hell, I can't even walk down the street without feeling like everyone's hating on me. I wake up with my chest so tight I can't breathe.

LETITIA: Yeah, I know that feeling.

JASON: I made a mistake. I know, I nearly killed somebody. I know, but I don't wanna be there again. I'm sorry, but everyone, including you, keeps telling me I'm shit. I'm shit.

CLYDE: And that's my fault, because—

JASON: Does it make you feel better to dump on us?

CLYDE: As a matter of fact, it does.

JASON: Well, you're . . . you're . . . you're mean!

LETITIA AND RAFAEL: Oooo.

(A moment. Clyde turns to Letitia.)

CLYDE: What did he say?

LETITIA: I think he said you're . . . *(Whispered)* mean!

CLYDE: No, I'm in charge. It's the thin line between being a productive member of our community or just another felon picking scraps outta the dumpster. Remember who helped all of you climb out of your shitholes. Do you know what I've sacrificed to keep this place open, to not be pulled back down? No, you don't, because you wouldn't know. I have more battle scars than most veterans. My life is a list of indignities that would make your skin crawl. Talk to me about cruelty, and I'll teach you something about perseverance. This world is mean, I'm just in it. Oh, you're quiet and moody now. I like that.

(A moment.)

You see that Rafael, that's what happens when you overdose on testosterone.

(Clyde gets into Jason's face. Montrellous enters.)

MONTRELLOUS: Everything okay?

CLYDE: Tell me again what you said.

JASON: . . .
CLYDE: Huh?

(Jason balls up his fist, anger has peaked. He moves to punch Clyde, but Montrellous intercepts.)

MONTRELLOUS: C'mon. Don't. You don't need the trouble.

(They have a heightened moment.)

CLYDE: What do you want me to do with you?
JASON: I want you to let me do my job!
CLYDE: Yeah?
JASON: . . . Yeah!
MONTRELLOUS: Y'all breathe, we got work to do.

(They have a brief staring match. Finally, Clyde smirks, lights a cigarette, and blows smoke at Jason.)

CLYDE: You ain't worth it.

(She leaves. Rafael exhales.)

MONTRELLOUS *(To Jason)*: You good?
RAFAEL: Dang?!
LETITIA: Oh shit!

(Montrellous exits.)

RAFAEL: I can't believe I witnessed that! I thought you were gonna get killed. A dead man.
LETITIA: "What do you want me to do with you?"

(Rafael high-fives Jason.)

Damn that was some caucasity. I ain't never seen her shut
down so quickly.

RAFAEL: For real. Cuz, I can't believe it!

JASON: C'mon.

LETITIA: "What do you want me to do with you?"

RAFAEL: Yo, be careful. You awakened the dragon. She's going
to take you out!

JASON: Get outta here.

LETITIA: Don't get too puffed up. It's not like her to go away
and lick her wounds. She's out there recharging her bat-
tery. Trust me, she's gonna make our lives hell.

JASON: Shit, can't get any worse than it is.

LETITIA: Oh yes, it can.

JASON: Well, I already had a bad ass day. It rained last night,
and all of my stuff got soaked, and then when I woke up,
some drunk had swiped my tarp and my burner.

LETITIA: Where the fuck do you live?!

JASON: I camp out near the Pagoda on Mount Penn.

LETITIA: Seriously, why?!

JASON: What do you care?

LETITIA: I mean like, why?

JASON: Because it's easier than shuffling around the shelter
with those sickos. Okay. I don't gotta talk to anybody.
Cuz, I'm talked out.

LETITIA: You ain't got nobody you can stay with?

JASON: There's my mom, but she's strung out.

LETITIA: I know how that is.

JASON: I feel safer out in the woods. And it's nice and quiet
at night. Smells good. And my mom's got some fuckin'
guy hanging around, I don't like 'em. I know me and him
gonna get into it. And I'm not looking to give 'em reasons
to trip me up. I see guys come out, and like a month later
they're back in cuz of petty shit.

LETITIA: Word. My ex. Keith. When I got released I thought we could, you know, work it out. I thought he'd be all happy and whatnot. Ten days home, it became real obvious that he had no interest in being a lover, being a parent, being a participant in our lives. Only thing he was interested in was getting and staying high.

RAFAEL: I know all about that. You want me to talk to him? I can—

LETITIA: It ain't even worth the saliva.

RAFAEL: Sure it is.

LETITIA: You're sweet, isn't he sweet? But, let me tell you something I learned real quick when I got out. People like Keith don't give a shit about anything. First sign of hardship and they wanna straddle you with their misery. All they see is the fucking black hole looming out there. And rather than moving away from it, they let themselves get sucked right in. A black hole. I seen that shit on television, and it's scary as hell, you know what's in a black hole?

RAFAEL: Nothing?

LETITIA: That's right, mutherfucking nothing. Everything that gets sucked into it gets trapped, light, gas, mass. And you know the problem with a black hole?

JASON: Nah.

LETITIA: It grows larger, it sucks you in and consumes everything around it. That's the truth. I used to be one of those people stuck in the gravitational pull. But, being incarcerated taught me two things: Number one, I love freedom, and number two, you have to fight to protect your freedom—

RAFAEL: Yo.

LETITIA: Truly. Back then, I didn't get it. I was the most finger-pointing bitch you'd ever encountered. My negativity was legendary. I could pass blame like a magician. Everyone was responsible for my unhappiness but me. And that darkness is still there, but now I can see that I can't let it or anybody get ahold of me. I'm being one hundred percent serious. But, that hole's pullin' atcha, and you don't even know it. Cuz you've been wearing that white-ass male privilege for too long, it's like blinders keeping you in the darkness. But, I bet you understand something right now, prison is the great equalizer.

RAFAEL: Fuck, yeah. They strap a bag of rocks to your back, and won't never let you put 'em down.

JASON: Shit is true.

RAFAEL: Too true.

LETITIA: True. *(Whispers)* Black hole. Fight the gravitational pull.

(Rafael flips food on the grill.)

Us, here. We're the resistance!

RAFAEL: Viva La Resistencia!

(Rafael raises his spatula in the air. Jason allows himself a smile. Transition.)

SCENE 11

Salsa blares. Rafael dances to the music on the radio as he preps a sandwich.

Jason rolls his eyes, finishes making a sandwich, and rings the bell.

JASON: Can we turn this shit off. It's giving me a headache.

(Jason changes the radio to a hard rock station. Rafael turns it back.)

RAFAEL: This is my jam!
JASON: Rafael. Give us a break! I can't hear myself think!

(Rafael teasingly dances.)

RAFAEL: You guys. Too serious. C'mon, I'm happy, I'm feeling life! I see your hips moving, mami.
LETITIA: Oh be quiet.

RAFAEL: Surrender to the beat. Friday night. I'm taking you out. Watch and wait. You're gonna fall in love. Love. Love. Love.

(Rafael dances around Letitia, she laughs.)

C'mon.

LETITIA: No. Stop. If Clyde catches us.

(Letitia allows herself to enjoy the moment with Rafael. They dance.)

RAFAEL: If Clyde sees these moves, she won't be able to resist.

(Rafael does a series of sexy moves. They haven't noticed that Clyde is standing in the doorway.)

I'll be like, "Clyde, come to papa."

(He pretends to be dancing with Clyde.)

CLYDE: Oh really?

(Rafael stops dancing. Paralyzed.)

Show me whatcha gonna do for me, Rafael. Come on.

(Clyde sways her hips, doing a more elaborate dance than Rafael.)

RAFAEL: . . . I was just playing.

CLYDE: Yeah? Maybe you should stop trying to play with the grown-ups.

(Clyde turns off the radio.)

I'm glad you guys have time to fool around, but I got my investors coming on Monday and I need you slack asses to be on your toes. Don't look at me that way, I'm not playing.

(Montrellous enters smiling. He carries a newspaper under his arm. He does a fancy showy spin. He puts on his hairnet.)

MONTRELLOUS: Good morning, people! . . . Remember this muthafucking day!

CLYDE: Oh, now you just come in when you want.

MONTRELLOUS: Before you saying anything. Read.

(Montrellous holds up the newspaper. He hands the newspaper to Clyde.)

Page five. Read.

CLYDE: Why?

MONTRELLOUS: Just read it.

CLYDE: Where?

MONTRELLOUS: Restaurant picks.

CLYDE *(Reading)*: "If you are driving along Old Pike Road, do yourself a favor and take a rest stop at Clyde's Sandwich Shop." Huh?

(Letitia screams. Joy.)

LETITIA: Oh my God. We're in the paper.

MONTRELLOUS: Read further.

CLYDE: "The place may seem unremarkable on the outside, but the long lines of truckers reveal the truth. The sandwiches in this greasy spoon are sublime."

LETITIA: That!

(A collective release of excitement.)

CLYDE: "Everything on the menu is excellent, but do try the Manuel Luis Echegoyen, which offers fabulous Latin flavors—"

RAFAEL: Yes!

CLYDE: "And the grilled cheese sandwich, which somehow elevates this simple classic to a masterpiece."

LETITIA: This is giving me life.

CLYDE: Well! Huh!

MONTRELLOUS: We have arrived! What did I tell you?

CLYDE: Huh?

LETITIA: Let me see that.

(Reading.)

Y'all!

JASON: Sublime. I know what that means! Can I see?

(Letitia passes him the newspaper.)

Sublime!

RAFAEL: We gotta frame this and hang it on the wall outside.

CLYDE: Don't let this go to your head.

MONTRELLOUS *(Grabbing the newspaper)*: This . . . this here is all of your hard work. They've seen us!

(Montrellous holds up the newspaper like a trophy. They hug. Collective excitement. This is a true moment of joy. Clyde watches, arms folded. She isn't sure what to feel. She grabs the newspaper from Montrellous.)

CLYDE: Okay . . . hmm . . . Okay . . . back to work. This feel-good moment's over.

MONTRELLOUS: Imagine what could happen with a new sign outside. A proper menu.

CLYDE: Ain't nothing wrong with the old one.

MONTRELLOUS: Put aside all the bullshit for a second, this is a real opportunity. You read it.

CLYDE: Don't get too high on hope. It's a blurb in a free newspaper that homeless guys use to wipe their asses. We're a bunch of felons making sandwiches. They don't mention that, but imagine if they did. Then, you think those fancy people are gonna flock from the hill for your food. C'mon be for real.

MONTRELLOUS: Why can't you let them have just a tiny bit of joy?

CLYDE: Cuz y'all know what you've done, and you don't deserve it. And a little salt and pepper ain't gonna make the truth taste any better. *(To Montrellous)* So, I suggest you put on your apron and remember why you're here. I'm not a fortune teller, but I can tell you this review is a baby aspirin, it won't fix a damned thing.

(These words hit Montrellous like a sledgehammer. Feeling triumphant, Clyde crumples the paper.
Rafael ventures to give Montrellous the paper, he rejects it.)

MONTRELLOUS *(With edge)*: You keep it!

(A moment.)

LETITIA: Yo, Monty—!

MONTRELLOUS: Look, I don't wanna get your hopes up for nothing.

LETITIA: But, we'll get there, right? Right?! Yo, you need to say sumptin'.

MONTRELLOUS: Honestly . . . I dunno.

(Montrellous stops himself, takes in the wounded faces of his coworkers. Dejected, he walks away.
Transition.)

SCENE 12

Jason prepares a sandwich. He is proud of his accomplishment.

JASON: I think I'm ready.

(Montrellous studies the presentation, contemplates, then takes a bite.)

MONTRELLOUS: Interesting. Grilled chicken. Mmmm, honey drizzle.

JASON: And, guess the surprise ingredient.

(Montrellous takes another bite.)

Yeah?

MONTRELLOUS: Swiss chard.

JASON: How'd you know?

MONTRELLOUS: It's bitter, assertive. Trying too hard.

JASON: So, you don't like it.

MONTRELLOUS: I didn't say that. You want it to do too much, and didn't trust yourself with the ingredients. They're at war. Let the natural flavors do the work. You put everything into this one sandwich. Edit. Pull back. Overcomplication obscures the truth.

JASON: Do you think Clyde's right?

MONTRELLOUS: Clyde answers to people who don't want us to succeed.

JASON: But, do you think it's possible that this place could become something?!

MONTRELLOUS: It could, but whether it will, that's an entirely different story.

(Jason smiles. He reveals the framed restaurant review.)

JASON: I got it framed. "Sublime."

MONTRELLOUS: Nah. You put it up someplace.

JASON: No. It's for you.

MONTRELLOUS *(Genuinely touched)*: Thank you, man.

(Montrellous examines the picture on the frame. He gathers strength from it.)

JASON: No, thank you. I hate that every time I look in the mirror I see all my shit on my face. But, when I'm here I kinda forget, don't think about it.

MONTRELLOUS: Yeah, I dig it.

JASON: You don't know what this means to me.

MONTRELLOUS: I do.

JASON: I had this whole fantasy of what life was gonna be like when I got out, thought it would be easier to leave all the bad shit behind, start where I left off . . . You wouldn't know it, but I had a good life going before I got incarcerated. I had an apartment in the heights, for real, a 401(k), then shit went south.

MONTRELLOUS *(Reflecting on Clyde's biting words)*: Ain't that how it always goes.

JASON *(Reflective)*: Yeah. I guess. I lost my job, got locked outta my factory by some greedy corporate assholes, and it felt like the world was over. Kept looking for people to blame. Anybody, everybody, fuck 'em all. And then when these . . . scabs started crossing the picket line like it was nothing, all I could think was, you can't have my vacation on Hilton Head, my Harley, my ice-cold beer after work, you can't fucking have it. And . . . I wanted to destroy 'em. I got drunk, like real drunk, found a bat in my hand and picked this one guy to release on.

(A moment. Jason speaks as if talking to the victim.)

I know I was wrong. I'm sorry. I'm so fucking stupid and sorry, and I hate thinking about it, cuz it hurts all of the time. I'm sorry. I'm so sorry.

(Tears.
Jason gives Montrellous an awkward hug.)

MONTRELLOUS: Hey. You wanna try that sandwich again?
JASON: Yeah.

(Letitia rushes in, catching the men in the hug.)

LETITIA: Oh . . .

(Jason pulls away and goes to his station.)

Sorry I was late. Had a night. My man surprised me with a cake, he never does shit like that.

JASON: I thought he was bad news.

LETITIA: Yeah he is. But, you know. Thirty! Y'all. This is what it looks like!

JASON: Happy birthday. I meant to get you something.

MONTRELLOUS: Happy birthday, baby.

(*Rafael enters, sullen, not his usual sunshine. He's not quite as put together as usual. He carries a teddy bear under his arm and a box of chocolates.*)

Hey.

RAFAEL: . . . hey.

LETITIA: Hey.

(*Rafael actively ignores Letitia.*)

What's going on?

RAFAEL: Nothing.

LETITIA: Sumptin's up!

RAFAEL: Leave it!

LETITIA: Yo—

RAFAEL: Leave it.

LETITIA: Yo!

RAFAEL: Step off!

LETITIA: Who you talking to?!

(*Rafael begins to make sandwiches. Messy. Angry.*)

Where's the love in your fingers?

(*Rafael gives her the middle finger.*)

Oh, you're gonna be that way.

RAFAEL: . . . You know, I waited for you.

(A moment. Rafael throws the teddy bear with the heart at Letitia.)

LETITIA: OMG. Was that last night?!

RAFAEL: Yeah. It was last night. Godiva!

LETITIA: I'm so sorry, I—

RAFAEL: No phone call or nothing. You ghost me?

LETITIA: I thought you was joking.

RAFAEL: Do I look like a fucking joker?

LETITIA: I'm sorry. Keith came over and surprised me with an ice-cream cake.

RAFAEL: Well, that ain't good enough. I had a whole dinner planned, roses, chocolates, the movies, everything. You know how much it cost me? My heart!

LETITIA: I'm sorry. I'll pay you back.

RAFAEL: I don't want your money. I want you to take me seriously. You're so used to that guy that don't treat you right, an ice-cream cake? Fuck that, I'm offering you something real.

LETITIA: You know how many times I've heard that. I'm tired of men! Maybe I don't want to give myself to anybody!

(Rafael rips opens the box of chocolates and shoves chocolates into his mouth. He smears the chocolate on his face.)

Stop that!

(Letitia tries to stop Rafael. He pushes her away.)

Then be that way. I thought you was joking.

(Rafael and Letitia don't say anything. Rafael's mouth is smeared with chocolate.

    Jason, eyeing the box of chocolates, goes to take one.)

JASON: Can I have a chocolate?

(Rafael grabs the box.)

RAFAEL: No!

(Rafael's behavior is erratic, twitchy.)

MONTRELLOUS: Everybody take a deep breath.
JASON: What's up with him?
LETITIA: Wait. Hold up! You been using Rafael?
RAFAEL: No!
LETITIA: Don't fucking lie to me. Look at me, have you been using?

(Rafael buries his face in his hands.)

RAFAEL: . . . A little bit.
LETITIA: There's no little bit. Either you have or you haven't.
MONTRELLOUS: Rafael! Brother, please tell me you haven't been using.
RAFAEL: . . .
LETITIA: So?! You wanna go back inside?!
RAFAEL: Who cares?
LETITIA: I fucking care! How could you?!

(Shaken, Letitia hits Rafael.)

How could you?! How?

(Letitia hits Rafael three more times, truly distressed. Montrellous stops her.)

MONTRELLOUS: Stop! Please! This ain't how we gonna do things.

(Montrellous pulls her away.)

RAFAEL: I waited for you.
LETITIA: I'm so sorry. Ain't nobody ever done something nice for me. I didn't want to be disappointed. I'm sorry.

(Letitia hugs Rafael.)

RAFAEL: I love you.
JASON: No! This is . . . too much for me first thing in the morning.
MONTRELLOUS: I think they need a moment.

(Rafael and Letitia continue to hug, deep, intense. Everything. Transition.)

SCENE 13

*A heightened moment of the crew using the kitchen activities to re-
store harmony. They have become more in sync, graceful, and pro-
ficient. The act of making food together is resurrecting their spirits.*

RAFAEL: Okay. Listen up. Grilled cheese, blue cheese, with
spinach, habaneros, and candied apples.

ALL: Yesssss.

LETITIA: Pulled pork, pickled onions, blueberry compote on a
soft pretzel roll.

ALL: Mmmmm.

MONTRELLOUS: Jason?

JASON: I dunno.

MONTRELLOUS: C'mon.

JASON: Um, grilled skirt steak sautéed in butter, thinly sliced,
caramelized onions, and peach chutney.

MONTRELLOUS: On?

JASON: A cheddar biscuit? A cheddar biscuit!

(They all applaud. Jason allows himself a moment of triumphant joy.)

LETITIA: Montrellous—
MONTRELLOUS: BBQ duck with—

(An order. Montrellous takes it, reads, rereads it. Furious.)

LETITIA: You okay, Monty?
MONTRELLOUS: Does that say relish?

(Jason reads.)

JASON: Yeah.

(Montrellous paces. He's furious.)

LETITIA: What's wrong?
MONTRELLOUS: I'm being tested? Nope! Not gonna do it!
RAFAEL: What's it say?
MONTRELLOUS: This fool wants pickle relish on the Manuel
    Luis Echegoyen.
RAFAEL: That's crazy. // Why?!
LETITIA: Hold up, that's bullshit.
MONTRELLOUS: Sacrilege!

(Montrellous puts his head in the window.)

No! I won't destroy the integrity of the sandwich!

(Clyde enters, fuming.)

CLYDE: What the hell are you yelling about?! You're taking too
    much time to make the sandwiches. This ain't *Top Chef.*

(She takes a sprig of parsley off the top of the sandwich.)

What is that?

JASON: A garnish.

CLYDE: Did you just say the word garnish?

JASON: Yes, it's a sprig of Italian parsley, it provides a tiny accent of flavor. We've noticed the truckers enjoy it.

CLYDE: I can't tell whether you're being serious.

JASON: I'm being totally . . . serious.

CLYDE: You melt American cheese on Wonder Bread and these truckers'll be happy. Hurry up! There's a line that snakes outside. Unacceptable!

MONTRELLOUS: That line's there because people want Italian parsley on their sandwiches. They want fresh thyme from my herb garden on the meatball sub, and they want the extra love that Rafael puts into the Echegoyen.

RAFAEL: Yup!

CLYDE: That was very touching, but I don't care. I want you to stop it.

MONTRELLOUS: And if we don't?

CLYDE: Hello. I'm gonna let you in on a little secret, I'm in debt to some real demons who will seriously punish us if we don't do what they want. And what they want is for us to keep our heads down and do our jobs. It's the deal I made, and we gotta live with it. And you, you keep your lofty ideas outta their heads, they're my . . . employees! *(Growls, reverberates)* MINE!

MONTRELLOUS: But, what if we turned this into somethin' we're all proud of? Huh? Something that defies expectations. Transcendent.

CLYDE: Don't hold your breath.

MONTRELLOUS: What if we endeavor to make each bite a trucker takes a sacred experience.

CLYDE: Look around. You're all losers, felons, fucking criminals.

JASON: // Speak for yourself.

LETITIA: I resent that.

RAFAEL: // I'm a sous-chef!

LETITIA: I did my time. Paid my debt. I'm many things, but I ain't a loser. I'm gonna be a real chef.

CLYDE: Don't disappoint me by having aspirations. Social hour's over. Pick up the pace, or tomorrow I can get a fresh batch of nobodies to do your job. And I'll make sure you go back to whatever hell you came from. Try me!

(Clyde leaves. They're all deflated.)

LETITIA: She wouldn't dare.

JASON: That's messed up.

RAFAEL: Yup!

JASON: Yeah it's garnish! Fuck you!

MONTRELLOUS: We all make our choices. You never know what-cha gonna do when you meet the devil at the crossroads.

JASON: I hate this place. If I wasn't in the bar that night trying to drink myself stupid, I—

RAFAEL: We've been there. We've all done things we ain't proud of.

LETITIA: Word.

MONTRELLOUS: But, we ain't bound by our mistakes.

(Montrellous has grown quiet and remote as he finishes the sandwich.)

JASON: What about you? I don't get why you're stuck here.

RAFAEL: // Yeah.

LETITIA: Yeah, you've never told us what you done.

(Montrellous places the sandwich in the window, rings the bell.)

MONTRELLOUS: I haven't? Don't talk about it much. A couple of you know, I'm the oldest of two brothers. My mom died when I was twelve and my father wasn't the saint you'd want at a time like that. He hit the bottle hard, then slowly disappeared, until one day he was just gone. So, it was me and my little bro Darius looking out for each other. And despite all that, Darius managed to do good in school, you know, get into one of those fancy prep schools, and then drag his ass through college working maintenance. He was a brilliant little dude. I watched in a constant state of wonder and admiration. Darius had one of those brains that could cut through bullshit like a laser, he knew from the time he was five exactly what he wanted. And me, I was trying to get through the day, and doing what you do to keep food in the fridge. Nothing more, nothing less. You feel me?

(Montrellous's voice gets tight with the emotion of the memory.)

Darius got into Yale Medical School on a full scholarship. No joke! I can't tell you how proud I was, honestly I thought my heart was gonna explode. Cuz I know how hard he fought to get there. And then . . . three weeks before entering medical school, Darius was hanging out on the hill with some of his rich white prep school friends. And he caught a ride home with this teammate, Brad Larkin, his father wuz sumptin' important in, um, banking. This white boy asks Darius to hold a duffel bag for him overnight. And being the good dude that he is, Darius says, "No problem." Next day Brad calls up and asks him to drop the bag off at this bodega a few blocks from our crib. You know, Darius doesn't think anything about it, grabs the bag, slings it over his shoulder. Gets to this bodega, and the minute he walks in, there are something like ten cops on him.

LETITIA: That's wack.

JASON: What?!

MONTRELLOUS: Ain't it though. Turns out the bag is full of dope.

(Collective moan.)

Yup! His friend Brad disappears like a genie, his family won't talk, and my brother, who never even stole a cookie from the cookie jar, is looking at serious time. There was nothing he could say, nothing he could do, cuz he got caught holding the damn bag. And this punk-ass lawyer was pushing him to plea bargain and take five to seven years and shit. But, Darius wasn't going to surrender without a fight, and I knew the fight would break him. I knew that there was no way the system was gonna let this smart young brother go. I knew the fight would change him and that he'd never get to medical school, and that would be a fucking loss. Darius had to make it. At the time, and I'm gonna be totally honest with y'all, I wasn't in a good way, done some things I ain't proud of. Was smoking too much weed, moving from job to job trying to keep one step ahead of anything substantial, and I was well on my way to squandering a perfectly good life. Then this happened . . . and . . . um, when I saw Darius sitting in that jail, hardening by the day, that was it. I was gonna kill somebody. I was straight-up homicidal. Everything about the situation was wrong. I didn't know what I was gonna do, but I knew I had to do something. So I walked into the DA's office and told 'em that I'd given Darius the bag, the dope was mine and he didn't know nothing about it. I told 'em I was sorry, but I couldn't let him take the blame for something I'd done. Darius begged me, "Don't do it!" but I told 'em I was willing to carry the burden so he could succeed, and the only thing I wanted in return was for him to excel. I loved him, and I believed he had more to give to the world than I did at that moment. Didn't even go to trial, I copped a plea, did the time.

RAFAEL: And what happened to Darius?

MONTRELLOUS: He's a surgeon— //

LETITIA, RAFAEL AND JASON: Ooh!

MONTRELLOUS: —with Doctors Without Borders working in a refugee camp on the border of Chad and the Sudan.

LETITIA, RAFAEL AND JASON: Aah!

(Gentle gasps.)

MONTRELLOUS: He's saving lives every day, specializing in pediatric trauma surgery.

LETITIA, RAFAEL AND JASON: Wah!

(Letitia gasps, this information is almost too overwhelming.)

RAFAEL AND JASON: Holy shit!

MONTRELLOUS: Yes.

(Letitia, Rafael and Jason begin to cry.)

LETITIA: I knew you were dope. But that may be the dopest thing I've ever heard.

JASON: That's beautiful. How the fuck are we supposed to live with ourselves?! I feel inadequate in your presence. I'm the most selfish pig.

RAFAEL: Yo.

JASON: I mean, I could never ever do anythin' like that.

MONTRELLOUS: Of course you could. Can't be afraid of the hard choices.

(Jason absorbs this.)

JASON: Yeah. Yeah.

(Clyde reenters.)

CLYDE: What the fuck is going on back here?

(Clyde drops the sandwich on the counter.)

Where's my relish?!

(A moment.)

MONTRELLOUS: Not doing it.

CLYDE: It ain't your choice. I got my investor out front, he wants relish on his sandwich, so don't fucking embarrass me.

MONTRELLOUS: Well, it's an abomination. And I won't do it.

CLYDE: Really? Put relish on the goddamn sandwich!

(Clyde looks at the others.)

MONTRELLOUS: No.

CLYDE: Gimme a break.

MONTRELLOUS: I won't cross that line.

CLYDE: Rafael, put relish on this fucking sandwich.

(Rafael looks to Montrellous.)

RAFAEL: Sorry . . . I can't do it.

CLYDE *(To Jason)*: You. Don't tell me you've also been drinking the damn Kool-Aid? Tish.

(She shakes her head.)

LETITIA: No!

CLYDE: Someone put relish on that fucking sandwich! NOW!!!

(None of them move. Clyde makes a big show of opening up the quart jar of relish, scooping out relish, and putting a huge glob on the sandwich.)

You're all replaceable! Get that into your head! Replaceable.

MONTRELLOUS: We're not replaceable, but we can be replaced.

CLYDE: There's something seriously wrong with you. All of you! I will be back to deal with this!

(She storms out of the kitchen with the sandwich. Montrellous prepares another sandwich.)

MONTRELLOUS: What could I have done? I made that sandwich with thoughtfulness, intention. It was an intervention.

JASON: That was very brave. The other day a trucker asked me to put ketchup on his tuna salad, and it made me sick. But I did it Montrellous, and I feel ashamed. I did not have your resolve.

MONTRELLOUS: I understand.

(Montrellous continues his sandwich.)

RAFAEL: Yo, Monty, what's your favorite sandwich?

MONTRELLOUS: Hm. I guess I crave the perfect harmony of ingredients.

LETITIA: Do you think a perfect sandwich can be made?

MONTRELLOUS: Perhaps, or will it just awaken another longing. Let's see.

(Montrellous completes the sandwich. Satisfied, he places it on the center of the table.)

He takes off his hairnet, his apron and puts on his street hat. Just before he leaves, he rings the pick-up bell. When he exits, it is as if there has been a gentle rip in their universe, allowing him access to a new realm beyond the confines of the kitchen [limbo].

Jason, Letitia and Rafael aren't sure what to do. Rafael adds a carefully considered sprinkle of salt on the sandwich, takes off his bandanna, and leaves. Letitia gracefully adds a dab of her special sauce, takes off her hairnet, and leaves. Finally Jason thoughtfully places two sprigs of parsley on the sandwich. Satisfied, he removes his hairnet and leaves.

A moment later, Clyde peers through the pass-through window.)

CLYDE: Montrellous!

(She enters the empty kitchen. She sees the sandwich, and her first impulse is to throw it, then she examines it. Considers. As she raises the sandwich to her mouth, she smiles, and then a large flash of fire surrounds. Blackout.)

END OF PLAY

LYNN NOTTAGE is a playwright and screenwriter, and the first woman to be awarded two Pulitzer Prizes for Drama (for *Sweat* and *Ruined*). Her plays have been produced widely in the United States and throughout the world. Her works include *Clyde's*; the musical adaptation of *The Secret Life of Bees*, with lyrics by Susan Birkenhead and music by Duncan Sheik; the opera adaptation of her play *Intimate Apparel*, composed by Ricky Ian Gordon; *Mlima's Tale*; *Sweat* (Pulitzer Prize, Obie Award, Evening Standard Award, Susan Smith Blackburn Prize); *MJ the Musical*; *By the Way, Meet Vera Stark* (Lilly Award); *Ruined* (Pulitzer Prize, Obie Award, Lucille Lortel Award, New York Drama Critics' Circle Award, AUDELCO Award, Drama Desk Award, Outer Critics Circle Award); and *Intimate Apparel* (American Theatre Critics Award, New York Drama Critics' Circle Award).

She developed and curated *This Is Reading*, a multimedia performance installation in Reading, Pennsylvania; and *The Watering Hole*, a multimedia performance installation at the Signature Theatre in New York City.

Her television credits include *She's Gotta Have It* (writer/producer, Netflix) and *Dickinson* (consulting producer, Apple TV).

Her honors include the PEN/Laura Pels Master American Dramatist Award, the Doris Duke Artist Award, a Literature Award from the American Academy of Arts and Letters, the MacArthur "Genius" Fellowship, a Guggenheim Grant, a Lucille Lortel Fellowship, the Steinberg "Mimi" Distinguished

Playwright Award, the National Black Theatre Festival's August Wilson Playwriting Award, and a Lucille Lortel Sidewalk Star, among many others.

She is the co-founder of the production company Market Road Films, an associate professor in the Theatre Department at Columbia University School of the Arts, and a member of the American Academy of Arts and Letters, the American Academy of Arts and Sciences, and The Dramatists Guild.

Theatre Communications Group would like to offer our special thanks to Diane C. Yu for her generous support of the publication of Clyde's *by Lynn Nottage*

DIANE C. YU has been President and Chair of the Board of Directors of the Oregon Shakespeare Festival since 2019. She served on the Soho Rep Board for nine years and is a member of the National Council for the American Theatre. Yu is the former Deputy President of NYU and previously practiced law in California and Missouri.

Other TCG books sponsored by Yu include:

Cambodian Rock Band by Lauren Yee